## About the Author

Laurie writes and works in the community of Prince George, British Columbia. Some of her most favorite things to do include: gardening, playing with her five grandchildren, and writing poetry. Laurie began composing poems at the age of nineteen after starting an undergraduate degree in English literature. This is her first collection of poems to be released.

# Lovely Dysfunction

**Laurie-Ann Dillman**

# Lovely Dysfunction

Olympia Publishers
*London*

**www.olympiapublishers.com**
OLYMPIA PAPERBACK EDITION



A CIP catalogue record for this title is available from the British Library.

ISBN: 978-1-80074-314-4

This is a work of fiction.
Names, characters, places and incidents originate from the writer's imagination. Any resemblance to actual persons, living or dead, is purely coincidental.

First Published in 2023

Olympia Publishers
Tallis House
2 Tallis Street
London
EC4Y 0AB

Printed in Great Britain

# Dedication

This book is dedicated to each person in our world who is called to make it their life's purpose in some way or another to support a child who is fighting cancer. All of the proceeds from the sale of this book are being donated by the author to BC Children's Hospital in support of sick children's well-being.

# Acknowledgements

The author wishes to thank Olympia Publishes for their support and patience during the publication process of this book.

# *Introduction*

Several of the poems in this manuscript were written during my residency at Royal Roads University. As a result, the imagery in this manuscript reflects many of the thoughts and feelings that I had about personal development and the changes that came with the realization that if one imagines the world in a certain way, one must believe with all their might in that vision, to allow the universe to expand and make it so.

## *Masterpiece*

Break, break, break,
At the heart of thy matter, my enchanting love
Your existence was a simple masterpiece, and happily
lived aloud on plains and levels below and above.
Its design and fate intertwined
Guided by an unwavering belief in this world
your sweet heart sang a simple solo, and
willfully, you orchestrated away all but the good!
Now merely an image, you're alone in my tears, as
gallantly the sunlight caresses our faces
engraving your rich memory on this world, and
fearlessly, applauding your delicate graces.
Break, break, break,
At the essence of the universe, my passionate love
Let's agree to meet as souls in the breeze, and
living, yes alive, dance on plains and levels below and
above.

# *A Safe Place to Watch the World Burn*

I am right

Right, I know I am

Am I wrong? What if this is not who I am?

Who I think I am is not who will carry me

Carry me and us; I have so many questions that need sustainable answers to right now.

Right now, if I meditate quietly, I will remember what it is I must know

I must know if it's too late

Too late, I see them descending on me now, but I am unsure if I have the answer they need to know.

Knowing is everyone's business, what should I tell them?

Tell them not to hide, or retreat, or admit defeat

Defeat happens when we resist the one true answer

The true answer is yes, but only for us

For us: you and I

I will remind them to remember the way back

Back out, who me? I am nothing if not brave… I am nothing if not brave… I am nothing if not brave…

Bravely, I make eye contact

Contact is a satisfying conscious emotion.

# *The Humble Politician*

Under a sun colored golden gold among leaders of
nations and IGOs
There's a humble politician, both brave and bold,
translating the voices of faces unknown
Armed with the Law of Integrity, she hastens to hold the
conviction to deliver on matters untold.


Tenderly, her constituents are approached to be polled
Through the system of democracy, she challenges
what's sold.
Teaching the Principle of One: a theory of old: simply
gathering the world in half with a fold.


So, together by a fire and lost to the cold,


equality can begin without dice being rolled
new leaders can emerge by breaking the mold
to reveal a path leading to an unimaginable world.

# *Unity*

Dance, dance wherever you may be
Open up your mind to let your light shine free
Gaze into the heavens; what is it you see?

The universe reminds us as we journey, live and breathe
How unity expresses through connected groups of three
As we learn from all life's lessons throughout eternity.

The mistakes that we make only matter externally
Pay attention to the sequence; counting one, two, three
Hidden in plain sight over mountains, lands and seas.

Consider first your power in matters of equality
As you search for certain knowledge, praise all the birds
and bees
When sharing all this nectar, love genuine and sweet.

Meet others in the middle; agree to disagree
Recognizing that as humans, it's our responsibility
So, necessity and suffering can lead to peace and
harmony.

# *Constructed Structuring*

Searching in the directions of north, east, south and west
Using another's pathway; well-known at best.
Corporate leaders are attempting to construct and then
bypass all the tests.
Enticing stakeholders to pursue blindly along in their
footsteps.
To meet these agendas, society believes and invests
Using impartial systems designed by the best, we
wander and weave, forgetting to rest.
To go north is to commit to a higher road
Where conception is required and decisions… untold.
To go east toward the sun excites a new beginning
Despite that, the terrain's been charted; from beginning
to ending.
To go south is always the trendy choice
Likely you won't be alone; so remember to exercise
your voice.
To go west, young woman, the days are quite long
The wilderness quite vast, and its inhabitants quite
strong.
A corporate direction requires a good look around,
no flitting about, base it on decisions which are sound.
To erect one's mission on sacred ground is clear, my
dear, as the wisest leaders have found.

## *Follow Your Path*

We are always right where we need to be
in plain sight, yet somehow, it's not always easy to see
Our path draws us in from the moment we're born
And though they are crossed by many, they never
seem worn.


In our mother's womb, we prepare to meet
the ones we will cherish and the ones we will defeat.
With each new scene that is orchestrated by our
conscious minds
we get to taste; feel; touch; hear; and define
our fears; limitations; dreams; and desires
while quietly, the universe expands and
aspires, providing the space that our lives will
require from the moment we are born until the last
breath we expire.
Always these secrets are kept between
you and I
The reasons we exist and the
reasons we die
Yet, there is a place we can go right here on this
earth
to be reminded of our purpose and acknowledge our
worth
The way is imprinted in us to remember our whole
life through

no matter where we go or the things that we
choose to do
Pay attention, pay attention, pay
attention, we're told
for at this exact moment,
we hold
in our hearts and our heads, a choice
whether to resist the way or add
our voice
It's not luck that decides when we are ready to find
that our path leads the way from in front and
behind
It is love that defines our desire to belong
for without it, there's no use for values of
right and wrong
When we live to raise up others
as demonstrated through our parents
our fathers and mothers
we become like drops of rain flowing out
to the sea
never alone and always right
where we need to be
It is when we surrender to
the way
that our lives start to flow
and our hearts become free.

# *Bring Along Your Thoughts and Words*

Around the world, we live our lives
from birth to death and earth to skies
Past generations needing space;
explored this planet seeking grace
Not knowing all there was to see,
they ventured forth to live their dreams;
Meeting strangers one by one,
sharing cultures, erasing some
Each country gained, with passing years,
greater values and lesser fears.

Of meaning held within our hearts,
there beats the will to be a part
Identity, religion, music, dance and race
all exist to set a culture's tone and voice
Traditions give us worth and fun
and ways to celebrate the work that's done
A need to manage, own and rule
has given birth to reckless tools;
But, don't be sad or shed a tear,
you're safe within your culture, dear
Listen carefully, as now is right
to spread your wings and take to flight
Bring along your thoughts and words;
please ensure your voice is heard.

Pray for laughter, dance in the rain
while letting go of needless pain
Rest your thoughts on fallen men;
only every now and then.

Believe in life, of what may come;
forever revolving, like the sun
Trust in knowing life's on track
because the universe has your back.

# *My Dearest Emily*

I watched you from my heart today; near the place where our friends, the seagulls, float and sway. You sat alone with a brush in hand to sketch a scene of Mother Nature's plan. Etched between the earth and sky, you gazed and then bowed at the youngest Monarch fluttering by the place where yesterday's cherry moon danced across this old lagoon. With every stroke of leaf and tree, I silently cherished you praising land and sea. Blue, yellow, red, green and gold, now breathe within your canvas bold.

Once I leaned a little close and sensing my light, you slightly froze. Stepping back, I returned your space, releasing a smile onto your face. Upon the shore, some strangers came. The clothes they wore were not the same. Out of their grandly-boat of steel and wood, they fetched their things and restless stood. Sensing friendship, the dogs drew near, eager for a scratch or two behind the ear. Words of few they shared with you, then off they went away.

Needing a stretch, you tossed a stick, the dogs would fetch out into the bay. Now the time has come, your canvas is done, and we're losing the light of day. So, I'll say goodbye and gently sigh, I miss you, it's been eighty years today.

All my love,
LD

# *Big Hard Sun*

The path is unknown, yet there's surety amidst each
turn. Because the journeys we walk unfold surprises to
learn. As time slips away from the beating heart
                              To understand is to
                    imagine our suffering as art.


Sharing with family and friends true emotions
          the values we cherish that arise through
faithfulness and devotion
     Outside there's a big hard sun and millions of people
                    who yearn
for their voices to matter, so they exist, and they burn.


                              A human
                    understands though
                    foolish, we are smart
          Raising up others requires true love from
                    the start
While standing one's ground takes more than a notion
          Like artists, we wield tools and systems for
sculpting kind acts of devotion
Tough decisions can be made so respect may be earned
          Until our purpose is lived and our work is
adjourned.

Nevertheless, the path is revealed together to the world
in parts
Allowing us to examine our suffering through art.

# Love and Intersectionality

Once upon a time, in a land not so far way
Lived a goddess with beautiful dark hair and skin
Brightly in her perfectly darkened domain she embraced
each day
Along with other goddesses, her only known kin.

Innocently shining on the other side of the world
Was a lonesome sun god, remarkably brave and bold
Wanting to share his internal desires; vast and uncurled
Embracing this purpose, he set out to brighten, we're
told.

Two worlds collided, legend says,
the moment this revolving god came within
All treasure forgotten as she asked him to stay
Recognizing in this moment that her heart was his to
win.

Since this story's been told
Many battles have been fought, many arrows been
hurled;
Many gods and goddesses grown old
Many generations of sunrises unfurled

Men have become Kings, on battlefields, they play

Knowing no right and no wrong- in doing so, forgetting
an original sin
One God's creation of love, providing their way
Remembering in time, how Intersectionality would
begin.

# *Six Years and Twelve Steps*

A six-year-old laughs and plays
atop a staircase… just yesterday
At the bottom of this staircase,
there's a glass-paneled door
All she has to do is reach the lower floor…

It is twelve brave steps from here to there:
defiantly, she descends them, stair by stair.
She hears his mother calling out her name
Should she turn back or finish out this game?
Through the shielding glass, she spies a bluebird
perched upon a tree
In her mind, she starts to wonder what to ask of thee.

Through the entrance left open-wide,
she boldly skips from side-to-side
Her mother's voice is far away:
forgotten now, she's lost in play
The bluebird watchful as she hops and skips
But flies off frightened when first she trips
Back through the glass door, no longer free,
her mother waits on bended knee
Twelve small steps are all she sees
Between herself and what she needs.

## *The People Gardener*


To grow a garden of people or beans
The way is the plan shared tools become means
A system is built as support and to lean
With
Ancient teachings exist to leverage the goal
A gardener steps up to nurture the whole
This true-hearted person believes from their soul
In
The seeds that are planted;
grow stems, flowers and leaves
Mother Nature assists; willingly,
with water and sunshine, she weaves
Until everyone who's watching sees and believes
Magically, the circle of life begins to unfold
This system of learning is ours; to have and to hold
"Pay attention, pay attention, pay attention," we're told
Our
Desires and our needs bait the Law of Attraction
Understanding this rule brings all kinds of satisfaction:
Remember, the universe grants
through small well-focused
Actions

# Blank Inside

These people are blank inside: today, you can feel free
to say whatever you like
Try speaking directly into the mic
Organize your thoughts so your words come out right
or left, no matter, these people are blank inside
Some people already have verses inside them
these are not those people these people are blank inside
Of course, they can hear you. Can't you see they have
ears?
They have no questions to ask as they are blank inside,
sometimes, it's better this way
There are no wrong answers you can provide: right now,
you can say whatever you like
Yes, they are here to listen to you: you are the expert
After today they will no longer be blank inside, and you
will need a new audience.

# *Stain Removal*

If I had earned a penny for every time I heard that
phrase, I would have earned a million dollars
Types of stains:
Religious, cultural, natural, relational, habitual, blood
Brief solutions:
Logic, order, patience, language, meditation, pandemics
Work inside out
To get out the stain try rebooting yourself
using a brief solution
Apply stain remover by working from the inside out
React quickly!
Apply stain remover as soon as possible
Warning!
Thoughts, emotions and tears
may permanently set stains.

## *When the Teacher Is Ready the Student Will Appear*

Find all the value in evaluation
Why must we rate our teachers on such a small scale?
One-to-five is highly irrelevant to common sense.

The purpose of life and all creation
The purpose is personal, possibly teachers never fail
Even in silence.

What can be learned from a student's summation?
How much is near truth, and what is tale?
Am I to judge for strength or incompetence?

Feedback is a gift that brings elation
So long as you obligingly respect the chosen grading
scale and
Knowledge and order stay in sequence.

# *Faith*

If you are reading this poem, you are right where you
need to be
The message I lend to you in this moment is one that
you have been waiting for all of your life
Congratulations! You are finally ready to receive it
Everything is going to be ok
Everything is as it should be
Everything happens for a reason
The beauty is that you are hearing it
presently  in this moment.

# *Just Breathe – An Ode to the Tao de Ching*

Of meaning held within our hearts, there beats a will to
be a part of…
"Being deeply loved by someone gives you strength,
while loving someone deeply gives you courage."
Of meaning held within our hearts, there beats a will to
be apart
"Compassionate toward yourself, you reconcile all
beings in the world."
Of meaning held within our hearts, there beats a will to
be a part of…
"Knowing others is intelligence; knowing yourself is
true wisdom."
Of meaning held within our hearts, there beats a will to
be apart
"Mastering others is strength; mastering yourself is true
power."
Of meaning held within our hearts, there beats a will to
be a part of…
"A good traveler has no fixed plans and is not intent on
arriving."
Of meaning held within our hearts, there beats a will to
be apart
"When you are content to be simply yourself and don't
compare or compete, everyone will respect you."
Of meaning held within our hearts, there beats a will to

be a part of…
"When I let go of what I am, I become what I might
be."
Of meaning held within our hearts, there beats a will to
be apart
"Because one accepts oneself, the whole world accepts
him or her."
Of meaning held within our hearts, there beats a will to
be a part of…
"A person with outward courage dares to die; a person
with inner courage dares to live."
Of meaning held within our hearts, there beats a will to
be apart
"Stop thinking, and end your problems."
Of meaning held within our hearts, there beats a will to
be a part of…
"A leader is best when people barely know she exists."
Of meaning held within our hearts, there beats a will to
be apart
"At the center of your being you have the answer; you
know who you are and you know what you want."
Of meaning held within our hearts, there beats a will to
be a part of…
"Other people have purpose; *I alone* don't know."
Of meaning held within our hearts, there beats a will to
be apart.

# *Hate the Sin, Love the Sinner*

I have heard it said through another's voice
There is universal hope for our human race.

Judging from his character and certainment
I asked of him how we shall allay all this detriment.

The conversation that happened next
Brought a certain lightness inside my breast.

Music sang within my ears
A playful mist released as tears.

The child within began to dance
Forgiveness and love, he says, is how to advance.

We must overcome the sins we perform
Forgiveness and love help us resist social norms.

# I Left My Memories in My Other Pants

My knowledge and knowing is ripe for the showing
But I left my memories in my other pants
My vocabulary and pretense is growing and growing
They asked me to speak; perhaps I know what they
want.

My storage if full; my cup's overflowing
A voice inside me is starting to rant
The things that I'm thinking are all wretchedly mind-
blowing
Yet my mind is insisting, as I'm resisting the dance
"They need me immensely," I'm certain, I heard myself
crowing
Letting go of this banter; means taking a chance
Perhaps before long, an Honorary Doctor of Law they'll
consider bestowing
Forgetting is part of unlearning the past.

Before future generations will want some of my DNA
for cloning
I must determine my purpose real fast
As somehow, I know there are infinitely more things for
the knowing
That's why I'm reminded not to store memories in my
pants.

# *The Jailbird*

I found a "get out of jail free" card
It was just lying there on the ground
No one was around, so keeping it wasn't hard
But what was I to do with this appealing thing I had
found?
Lost in my actions, my memory was jarred
So, lost in unknowing, I wandered around.

Days turned to months, months turned to years of
standing on guard
One day frustrated and unhappy, I was reminded of
something profound
And out of the blue, I fired my guard
And before long, I began living unbound
For the bars that had held me with unloving regard
Melted away like bubbling lard.

# *A Tale of Christmas in Kind*

Late this year, I looked into the mirror, and what did I
find?
but another new wrinkle of the arduous kind
brought about no doubt from continuous gardening
amidst the welcoming summer sunshine
Enough about that, though, here's a poem to playfully
amuse you using alliteration and rhyme.

The year started out with a contract I signed
As fortune would have it, my goals intertwined
With a college in Kelowna: so committing to deliver
instructions designed
I supported new learners whose furtive goals were
outlined.

Graciously, the gifts of the region helped me un-wine-d
When I connected with Sommeliers carefully tasting
their brine
After class, that is, never-you-mind
As a college instructor, I felt the need to refine.

Upon completion, I returned to my home where I was
Covidly-confined
But celebrate I did anyways, refusing to pine
As the proud grandmother of five (someday maybe

nine)
I managed quite easily, I tried not to whine.

Norah, Lucas, Avery, Myles, and Rylee supplied
Enough giggles and smiles combined
Thanks so much to Snap Chat, Instagram and especially FaceTime
I received much love, but mostly in-kind.

This Christmas, I consider myself blessed and am fully resigned
To resist sharing germs or risk getting fined
While the country awaits our politicians to align
And scientists to create vaccines to assign.

Naturally, the universe has provided many gifts that remind
Us of what life can be like, if we're all so inclined
To reflect, for a moment, on the suffering of our everyday grind
By embracing the silence, that brings peace to our lives.

# *Bloody-Tender Thoughts I Bleed*


These bloody-tender thoughts I bleed
To wash away my sins and deeds
Fall from grace-like eyes; blinded by countless
unforgiving needs
As believed in the hearts and minds of those I've dis-
eased
Re-lived, forever and ever amen; throughout all eternity
When I stand alone at Peter's Gate to humbly plea
May God forgive me of this added pain and suffering
I've devilishly multiplied throughout my time as a
human being.

# *Equanimity*

Mastering intent
Intently mastering peace
Peacefully content.

# *Hatley Castle*

The drapes are drawn, the world awaits
I am living in a fairy-tale
My chair is lush and sinks right down
From the weight of this royal crown
Out to sea, I cast a glance
A traveling ship? There is a chance…
A mighty Tamarac shares my gaze
As we both look upon the wondrous ways
Mother Nature teases, laughs and plays
Conducting every sunshine ray
As moments revolve into a day
The moon peeks out and asks to play
It's time to mate, the peacocks say
We could use less rain the gardener prays
I climb the stairs, one by one
Up to my room; the day is done
A roaring fire burns to warm my heart
While I dream of you until no more we part.

# *The Caretaker*


Once upon a church-filled day
There lived a man who loved to pray
Into the woods, he took his hound
Throughout the day, they wandered round
Praying here and praying there
They stopped to pray most everywhere
He praised the sunshine and the rain
And sometimes, he'd praise them all over again
All the bears and beavers too
Welcomed the man with softest shoes

All this time, no words were shared, yet the
conversation was truly rich
Whether among bee or frog, no matter which
Of all the wonders he did see
Near the waters, he preferred to be
Where nature's music filled his ears
And soothed away forgotten tears

When one day he came no more
A wreath was laid on nature's floor
The wind took stage and whispered loud
Across the valleys, prayers went out
Every animal, bird or bear
Took a breath of freshest air
In his honor, one by one
Christened by the noon-day sun.

# *Reflections*

Worries and fears of victims' past
beg us all to stop and ask:
Can peace exist in every heart
to help us cherish these broken parts?
Partnerships begin with two;
reconciliation exists in me and you
The ways of animals and yin and yang
show pathways through this sorrowful land
Protocols of faith mentor our souls;
teaching us how to share what's known-
inside the hearts of you and me
and gives us space to live and breathe
Reflections turn us inside out
to recognize ourselves no doubts
Love of others can make us strong
Knowing happiness comes with having the courage to
reflect, accept and carry on.

# *Separation*

Face-to-face in an open space
full of flowers and of grace
Force, thrill of powers in one place,
not one found, not one chase
Light on light, we brightly skipped,
Mother and me, a memorable trip
Light's tender kiss, first taste on lips, love's saving grip
Swaddled within your tresses, I lay caressed half the
night and day
While softly singing, you wisely imprinted upon my
heart; the truth the way.

Grow, I did as inklings do who belong to you
Soon, surrounded by a sacred garden, I cautiously began
to toddle and move
Seeking sustenance and rest among the waves of
compassion flowing abundantly from your breast
Eagerly I tended Nature's garden desk, exploring
suffering and separation, both of love's great tests
Studying the past re-living breathtaking examples of
historical context
My soul gave in, my heart let go, my ego had me vexed
Quietly raising my voice to ask questions I thought
deserved your attention and concern
All of this activity I dedicated to the belief that I could

one day earn
A title, a purpose, a lofty degree to use to know others
whose existence I might someday meet
Until that moment whence I restlessly stood, searching
outward for more tantalizing emotions to greet
Once a wise child, somehow, I had grown up to
embrace "if only" fantasies
Descending down, you selflessly blessed my needs
hoping that in time I would return to thee.


Now existing as an ethical infant with selfish sins
bought to hide a growing ego erupting from inside
I tried to remember the way: using imprinted directions
once denied
Unconsciously began self-doubt
as it reached in to bring about
Emotions forming into place
to choose and use to remember our space
Ancient patterns of geometric lace
reminding meaning to show its loving face
This time has come my needs all sought, my seeds all
sewn, my dirty tears all cried
I can feel your thoughts within my mind, yet it's not my
head but my heart that tries to find
A way to bridge your light with mine: your laugh, your
dance, your voice so fine
The universe has it all planned out
but synchronicity of dominance silently shouts
The days of this mind have bloomed once again:
sprouting poetic imagery and rhyme.
Spoken to appreciate cherry blossom-scented memories
of a Mother divine

Masterfully transforming a conscious heart into a
butterfly delicately fine
and ornate fluttering toward you through teardrops: soft
as rain
Finally, letting go of this life
and all of its imaginary sights
To twinkle outward by your side as a star of wonder,
star of light eternally shining bright.

## *The Prayers of a Child*

A little child from heaven came.
To enlighten the world through love, some might say
Although his parents had grace and faith, somehow
together, they lost their way
Separated by their values and fears: their love for one
another crumbled away
As the child grew, despite a room full of toys and lots of
happiness and play
His parent's estrangement made him doubt his
worthiness, so he prayed:

Dear Father in heaven, I need you to stay
close by me forever and remind me the way
to light up the path, while my parents both stray
Hearing this, God sent out angels to ask the faithful to
pray:
For forgiveness to happen and faith be exchanged
between his mother and father that very same day.

# Let Us Not Waste a Minute

Earth to earth, ashes to ashes, dust to dust, typically
consisting of a soul lifted up by the wind in trust
To land where it must nourish a seed as it thrusts
upwards toward the earth's primal crust
Forming a shape of some such that will be recognized as
much, with any luck
As food, it's just
Humans tend to waste our time as we must
Uncover the answers to all that exists by dusk.

# *Zen*

After breaking camp, dawn erupted, forming golden-
haired ice jewels: kaleidoscoping lightly, methodically,
naturally, obligingly, presenting quite robust scenes the
universe vigorously, willingly, xenaciously, yielded
zealously.

# *You Complete Me*

I

As I sat contemplating my life, it became perfectly clear
that who I am is because of everyone here
As my mind dreamt of the journey onward into the great
unknown
a part of me recognized intuitively that the way would
be shown
While contemplating this life, I naturally thought of
those I had wronged
Instead of choosing to consider any shame or defeat: I
began to consider the ways I belonged.

II

During this lifetime, I have heard many messages from
teachers, spiritual leaders, poets and Saints
Advising me as I went in search of my purpose to
master selfishness using egoic restraint
Perhaps, at these times, I never truly understood the
deepest meaning behind their advice
But experience has a way of reshaping the mind:
Interestingly, mistakes are the price
As I began to revisit all those lessons so purposefully
taught
Once believing I had learned them completely: Finally
realizing that, in truth, I had not
Strange I may have seemed to others as I began

conversing to myself about this life's many lessons
Indeed, discussing the purpose of failure while I
acknowledged my regrets and transgressions.

III

Reflection uncovered how by helping enough people to
get what they wanted
I was undermining the universe's plan through the half-
filled motto I was flaunting
Something quite simple was missing by seeking
happiness outside of myself
often repetitiously acting instead of allowing the path to
reveal itself.

IV

I am who I am because you are who you are: we all
need one other: the way a child needs a mother
Everything is connected; hence, we are the one, and I
am the other
The significance of what I am trying to say is how you
complete me
and not just in a devoted kind of way, but utterly,
totally, and completely.

# *Raising Our Self as an Equal*

I.
The system of marriage serves several purposes.
The first impetus is so people can become devoted to
raising themselves as an equal
Equals raising up equals across the river of life
Losing sight of this intention often causes discontent
Because love is as powerful as a tide when it ebbs and
flows.
II.
Fear, not bold lovers, as marriage is not an adventure for
the faint of heart
Marriage is a journey for those who want to learn to live
selflessly in the company of love.
Life happens; it is orchestrated in ways that accelerate
our needs and our desires.
Life calls us to our knees and raises us up onto
mountain peaks at sunrise
Shared moments can be a gift, a reminder and a breath:
marriage is for sharing moments.
III.
Emotions move us onward en route to the soul's
objective
Left… right… left… right… left… right… left…
right… left…
When we start to travel in circles, we often lose the

way, keep to the way
The way is synchronous to the natural proposition of
marriage: we're told
The system of marriage is ours to have and to hold.